Watermark: {**An Explanation of Baptism**}

By Bob Franquiz

Watermark: An Explanation of Baptism

© Copyright 2007 by Fuel Media Group, Inc.

Library of Congress Control Number 2007902482

Fuel Media Group, Inc.
15305 N.W. 60th Ave. Suite 100
Miami Lakes, FL 33014

Edited by Sacha Kauffman and Chuck Musselwhite
Cover Design by Gus Beltrami
Cover Photo by Oscar Falero
Interior Design by Gus Beltrami
Back Cover Photo Oscar Falero
Printed in the United States of America

"And all who have been
united with Christ in baptism
have put on Christ,
like putting on new clothes"

GALATIANS 3:27 NLT

Contents

Introduction: {**Watered Down**}

Introduction: {**Watered Down**}

When I was Sixteen, I got my first car. It was a 1982 Volkswagen Rabbit. It ran on diesel gas and broke down more times than I'd like to remember. I remember the day I got it. I paid the owner $400 for this gold colored disaster, but you wouldn't have known from the smile on my face. My VW Rabbit brought me the thing that every teenager desires most: freedom. All I had to do was learn how to drive it. My problem was I didn't realize that the car was a stick shift. I had never driven a car that wasn't an automatic transmission, so when I hopped into the car I was met with a rude awakening. I put the key in the ignition, turned the car on, and the violent jerking that ensued made me think I was on an Amusement Park ride gone horribly bad. Noticing my plight, the "former" owner of my car got into the passenger seat and walked me through some simple steps to get my new car off of his property. He taught me what the clutch was and that this was vital to shifting gears. He explained how to hear when the engine was ready for me to shift gears and accelerate further. Needless to say, I stalled out several hundred times after that and burned out the clutch in less than a year. But today, I'm pretty good with a stick shift and that "baptism" into the world of manual transmission set me in the right direction and got me moving.

I know it might sound odd, but this is how I view the book you're holding in your hands. Let me be honest with you: I'm not a Theologian. A theologian is a really smart guy that writes weighty books that most normal people don't read. I am a Pastor and a Bible teacher, and I have tried my hardest to be more practical than profound. As I have spent the last several years in ministry answering questions about what baptism is, I thought it might be a good idea to produce a simple guide that could help young followers of Jesus learn the significance, meaning, and purpose of this basic, yet sacred act.

This little pamphlet is kind of like the ten-minute tutorial that the man who I bought my car from gave me.

It's a crash course in the basics for those who are wondering about what baptism is. Yet more than anything, I hope it is like a droplet into a still body of water. My prayer is that this little booklet will create a ripple effect that will lead into you entering the waters of baptism and identifying with Jesus in His death and resurrection.

Chapter One {**Watermark**}

Chapter One {Watermark}

People have weird tastes, especially when it comes to food. Some friends of mine took me to a restaurant in Coral Gables and it was awesome. But my first time looking through the menu was like reading a French dictionary. It was the kind of high-end restaurant that only Miami can give you. It was fusion style cuisine that blends Caribbean, Latin, and American flavors all on your plate. I wasn't too excited about it but, once I ordered, it was amazing. I knew I had chosen wisely because of all the dishes I sampled, the only dish I really loved was the one I ordered. I don't know if you've ever felt that way in a restaurant—like you somehow dodged a bullet. While everything else I tried was good, it wasn't what I'd want to spend my evening eating. That's what makes people individuals. We all have different tastes and likings. That's why there are some foods or combinations of foods that you love and you are the only person on planet earth who loves them. But there are other foods that if you had the choice, you'd pick rat poison over a plate of _____. For example, my wife loves the taste of Coke and milk mixed. I've tried counseling, therapy, interventions, but she still loves it. I think it's just plain nasty! If Carey has a Coke by itself, she'll put ice in it and wait for the ice to melt to water it down. For most people, that happens by accident, but she sets out to do it. I'm not immune to the weird factor either. I know it sounds disgusting, but I really like the taste of cough medicine. It seems disgusting, but when I get sick, cherry flavored Robitussin is all I need. Most people gag when they have to take cough medicine. I, on the other hand, have been known to chug it from the bottle from time to time.

But I'm always interested in other's tastes for varieties of life. Like I don't understand how people can pay money to watch a movie that's tragic. Most of us just need to get out of bed in the morning to experience that for free. If you want me to never see a movie, just say these words, "It's really sad." Case closed. This bird has flown. I'm done. If it doesn't have explosions, funny dialogue, or an epic adventure, count me out.

FOUR WEDDINGS AND FUNERAL

In light of that, I do have one weird thing about me that not many people understand. I like funerals. I know that sounds morbid because most people don't. In fact, they try to go a lifetime without attending one, but I like them. Now let me clarify before you label me as some kind of mental case. I like officiating funerals. I don't like it when people I love pass away and I'm not looking forward to being the name on the program at my own memorial service. Yet, as a pastor, two of my "extracurricular" activities are weddings and funerals. All pastors have a preference as to which they prefer. The problem is, I've never met anyone who likes funerals more than weddings…except for me. So the question you want to know is, "Why?" I'll explain by asking you a question: What do you remember the pastor saying at the last wedding you attended outside of the usual "I do" stuff? Don't remember? That is precisely my point. The pastor could have been reading the phone book and most of us would have never known the difference because no one cares what the pastor says at weddings.

But at a funeral, we are hanging on every word because we are looking for God in those times. Sometimes a simple Bible verse can be the difference between hope and despair. So I guess I like the role that I play in funerals better because I feel like I'm making a difference.

Now don't get me wrong, I don't like the sad part of funerals. In fact, I hate that part. I hate seeing people cry and saying goodbye to someone they love. It kills me inside. But I love the fact that people are really open to God in those moments. It shows us that we aren't immortal and we are going to see our Maker someday. In contrast, I don't hate weddings. I love the joy, the commitments that are made, etc… I appreciate the families (even the crazy ones) who want everything just perfect for this most special of days. In fact, I know there's a God because there's a phenomenon to me that is unexplainable. I have never seen an ugly bride. Every bride I have ever seen has been stunningly beautiful. I have seen plenty of ugly wives in my life, but never an ugly bride. That's why I wish I could fuse the joy of weddings with the sobriety of funerals. Maybe at our next funeral, we could all get an expensive ring as we ponder life and mortality. Or at our next wedding, we could mourn the death of two individual people and celebrate the birth of a new couple committing their lives to each other. But I guess that might be like mixing Coke and milk; separate they're good, but together it wouldn't have a huge mass appeal. Then I started thinking that there is a place where the two meet. An event that symbolizes death but celebrates commitment…it's called baptism.

Maybe at our next funeral, we could all get an expensive ring as we ponder life and mortality. Or at our next wedding, we could mourn the death of two individual people and celebrate the birth of a new couple committing their lives to each other.

THE WATERBOY

If you're like me, you might have a mixed up view of what baptism is because of your background or the church you grew up in. In my particular childhood tradition, baptism was something infants did to become part of a religion and ensure they would go to heaven. Yet when I became a Christian, I soon discovered that isn't exactly what the Bible teaches. What I want us to experience together is one of the most important events in history. It's a baptism service that took place at the Jordan River 2,000 years ago. This baptism had nothing to do with religion or a ritual that marked my place in heaven because I got soaked inside of a church building. Instead, it shows us what baptism really is: that baptism is the mark of a life committed to God. That's why any Christian would want to get baptized. Jesus commanded us as His disciples to be baptized so it would serve as an outward symbol of an inward commitment. It would put the world on notice that we were leaving our old lives behind and embracing the lives that God has for us. And it would serve as a memorial to us of the day we fully committed ourselves to God. That's why Jesus was standing on the banks of the Jordan River that day. He was there to show us what baptism was all about. So where does Jesus go to get baptized? Perhaps better put, to whom does Jesus go? He went to John the Baptist. To a man that was consumed by God and was leading others to be the same. It is here that we find our model of what baptism is and why it should be an element in the life of every person that desires to be a disciple of Jesus.

> Then Jesus came from Galilee to the Jordan to be baptized by John. But John tried to deter him, saying, "I need to be baptized by you, and do you come to me?" Jesus replied, "Let it be so now; it is proper for us to do this to fulfill all righteousness." Then John consented. As soon as Jesus was baptized, he went up out of the water. At that moment heaven was opened, and he saw the Spirit of God descending like a dove and lighting on him. And a voice from heaven said, "This is my Son, whom I love; with him I am well pleased."
> {MATTHEW 3:13-17 NIV}

My niece, Sarah, is like a daughter to me. It's amazing how much you can love someone even though they probably don't totally understand it. But I love spending time with her because she has developed an amazing sense of humor and she is really artistic. I was talking to her recently about her future and how when she goes to college she can live with Carey and I, and she can come and

She hasn't decided **if that's the right choice for her.** Luckily, I still have 12 years to talk her into it.

work at the church (a shameless display of nepotism at its best). So Sarah and I were having one of our conversations a few months ago and I asked her when she had lunch at school because I wanted to visit her someday. So she said, "Noon." A couple of weeks later, I was in the neighborhood and I decided to drop by and see her during her lunchtime. The only problem was, she was nowhere to be found. I talked to a teacher in the lunchroom and asked where the Kindergarten class was. She said, "Sorry, that class has lunch from 11:00 to 11:30." Then it hit me: She's five years old and that means she doesn't know how to tell time!

I think that's how John must have felt when Jesus showed up to be baptized. It was like asking him, "What time do you have lunch?" John is stunned and replies, "I can't tell time. You should be the one telling me when I have lunch!" But Jesus was modeling something for us. He was showing us what the heart of baptism is all about. It's the mark of a life committed to God. In the Jewish culture, people would wash in what was called a "Mikveh." This was a ritual bath where you would immerse yourself to be cleansed ceremonially so you could go and worship at the temple in Jerusalem. This was especially used as part of a ritual for those that were not Jewish and were converting to Judaism. They would be baptized as a sign of dying to their old lives and entering into a new relationship with Yahweh, the God of Israel. But there was a little problem—John was baptizing Jewish people. He was telling them to repent because the kingdom of God was at hand, and that their Jewish heritage wasn't proof that they walked with God. So these committed people were baptized to signify their desire to really walk with God. That's why the religious people were angry. Baptizing Jews was outrageous—it was also unheard of! He was the only person doing this. That's how John got his nickname: "Yohanan the Baptizo" or John the Baptist. Lest you think there's a denominational thing going on here, literally he was called John the Immerser.[11] The Greek has a word for immerse and another word for sprinkle. "Baptizo" means to immerse. If Matthew wanted to let us know that John sprinkled people, he would have used another word: "Rhantizo." I joke around with pastors who believe in sprinkling and I tell them that John was called the immerser, not "Rain Man."

Yet, Jesus wanting to be immersed was a problem for John. Remember John is telling people to repent, but Jesus had nothing to repent of. He's God. He doesn't have sins to confess or shameful deeds to wash away. This is why John was stuck like a deer caught in the headlights. I understand this feeling. I remember being asked to teach at a

Leadership Conference and my pastor introduced me and then sat down and started taking notes! I asked myself, "What's wrong with this picture?" I felt like a high school basketball coach teaching teenagers the fundamentals of the game and Shaquille O'Neal shows up and wants to be part of the class. You'd say, "I think you should teach me!" (Unless it was the day we were learning to shoot free throws.) But Jesus said, "I want to be baptized because it fulfills what God requires." Only then does John agree to baptize Him. The issue for Jesus was to obey His Father and do what was right. There is something that happens when a person makes a decision to be baptized. They aren't just deciding to get wet; they are dying to the old way of life and craving to live the abundant life that Jesus offers.

> Or have you forgotten that when we became Christians and were baptized to become one with Christ Jesus, we died with him? For we died and were buried with Christ by baptism. And just as Christ was raised from the dead by the glorious power of the Father, now we also may live new lives.
> {ROMANS 6: 3-4 NLT}

MAY I SEE SOME IDENTIFICATION?

Being baptized is about deciding to be numbered with the disciples of Jesus, not getting wet or performing some ritual. You see, people won't have a problem with someone coming to church occasionally. But you tell your friends that aren't Christians that you are getting baptized and they are going to think that you're taking this "Jesus" thing too far. Do you know why? Because they recognize how important baptism is even though many in the church don't.

> Therefore, go and make disciples of all the nations, baptizing them in the name of the Father and the Son and the Holy Spirit. Teach these new disciples to obey all the commands I have given you. And be sure of this: I am with you always, even to the end of the age.
> {MATTHEW 28:19-20 NLT}

Jesus links baptism with following Him. The issue isn't, "Can I still go to heaven if I'm not baptized?" The thief on the cross did, but he never had the chance to be baptized. If they took him down from the cross and said, "Yes, that robbery was just a misunderstanding. Please accept our deepest apologies and have a nice day." I'm going to go out on a limb and say he would have gotten baptized. The issue is if you are a disciple of Jesus, you will gladly obey Him in this simple, yet powerful act. I watch Christians go years without being baptized because they don't think it's a big deal. I say, "Jesus asks us to do this. That makes it a big deal!" Many times these are the same people who are praying about God's will because they don't know what to do. We're never going to figure out what God wants us to do if we haven't done what we know for sure He's already asked us to do. Some say, "Well, I was baptized as an infant?" So was I. But that's not what Jesus is talking about.

> **...Baptism is not a removal of dirt from your body; it is an appeal to God from a clean conscience.**
> {1 PETER 3:21 NLT}

I have pictures of my infant baptism and I wasn't appealing anything to God except for my lungs, because it looks like I was screaming the whole time. I don't remember it and it didn't signify anything in my life. So I personally cannot say I have obeyed Jesus in this area when that baptism was not of my own volition. I think sometimes we hesitate because we're scared.

Because there's something inside of us that knows something happens when we go into the waters of baptism. I can tell you from personal experience, people don't leave the same if they really mean it. People repent before God, declare their faith in Jesus, and commit to living out His purposes for their lives. I have had people hand me packs of cigarettes in the water just prior to them being baptized. They quit right on the spot – no patch, no gum, no hypnosis, nothing. It was just a commitment to live for God starting

I can tell you from personal experience, people don't leave the same if they really mean it.

from that moment. Once, during a baptism service, I had a man who wanted to be baptized hand me his cigarettes while we were in the water. This baptism was at the ocean, so I put them in my pocket because I felt that being a litterbug during a baptism wasn't the most spiritual thing to do. My intention was to keep them in my pocket until I got out of the water and then throw them out. Unfortunately, I forgot they were in my pocket. So I got home and later that afternoon Carey was washing the clothes I wore at the baptism and she found a soaked pack of Marlboro's in my pocket. She said, "Bob, is there something about you that I don't know about?" So I told her the story, we shared a smoke and went our merry way (just kidding). She threw them out. That's all…

But I believe something happens when someone who has prayed to receive Jesus decides to get watermarked by baptism. It shows their desire to live a revolutionary life by adding that element to their lives that Jesus and John had. I was baptized when I had been a Christian for about four months, but in 1999 I was in Israel at the very spot where John baptized Jesus and I had baptized 25 or 30 people who were part of our tour group. At the end of the baptism service, I asked the other pastors to baptize me because I believed God was calling me to do something great. He was calling me to come to Miami to start a church. I was enjoying a good life. I worked at a big church and ran a college full of students whose sole desire was to serve God. It was great. Yet I felt God stirring me and I couldn't shake it. So at that moment in the Jordan River, I did what Jesus did in that same spot. I decided to get consumed by God. I decided to live a life that wasn't comfortable, but instead was revolutionary. It's what God calls every person who calls Jesus "Lord" to do. He calls them to get watermarked and start a revolution in their world by starting one in their own lives first. It's at that moment that you will hear the words that Jesus heard. The words of your loving, heavenly Father who will look from heaven and say, "That's my son in whom I am well pleased."

Now as they went down the road,
they came to some water.
And the eunuch said, "See, here is water.
What hinders me from being baptized?"
Then Philip said,
"If you believe with all your heart, you may."
And he answered and said,
"I believe that Jesus Christ is the Son of God."
So he commanded
the chariot to stand still.
And both Philip and the eunuch
went down into the water,
and he baptized him.

ACTS 8: 36-38 NKJV

Chapter Two **{Frequently Asked Questions about Baptism}**

Chapter Two | **Frequently Asked Questions about Baptism** |

1 – WHAT ABOUT INFANT BAPTISM?

The Bible teaches us that

> *"Baptism is not a removal of dirt from your body; it is an appeal to God from a clean conscience."* (1 Peter 3:21NLT)

Throughout the New Testament, only adults were baptized. The reason is because the act of baptism represents a life that has been changed by God and reflects the decision of the person to follow Jesus. Infant baptism speaks more to the parents' faith than it does of the child's, and that is not the purpose of baptism. The command of Jesus to be baptized is about your personal relationship with God. So we believe that a person need be of an age that allows them to make the decision personally to obey Jesus in this act.

2 – WHAT IS AN APPROPIATE AGE FOR BAPTISM?

> *"Now as they went down the road, they came to some water. And the eunuch said, "See, here is water. What hinders me from being baptized?" Then Philip said, "If you believe with all your heart, you may." And he answered and said, "I believe that Jesus Christ is the Son of God." So he commanded the chariot to stand still. And both Philip and the eunuch went down into the water, and he baptized him. Now when they came up out of the water, the Spirit of the Lord caught Philip away, so that the eunuch saw him no more; and he went on his way rejoicing."*
> (Acts 8:36-39NKJV)

While the Bible does not address a specific age that is a minimum requirement for baptism, the real issue is really one of the heart. The passage quoted above gives us the requirement for baptism. It has nothing to do with age and everything to do with the condition of a person's spiritual condition. A person who understands that Jesus is the Son of God and has made a decision to follow Jesus is the perfect candidate for baptism. The age of the person is dependant on their ability to understand what they are doing in baptism. This could be at the age of ten for one person and at 14 for another. We believe that a person seeking to be baptized must understand what baptism is and know why they are entering its' waters. This cannot be an issue of religious duty or parental pressure, but instead a spiritual conviction resulting from a living faith in Jesus.

3 – WHO SHOULD GET BAPTIZED?

"Then Jesus came to them and said, "All authority in heaven and on earth has been given to me. Therefore go and make disciples of all nations, baptizing them in the name of the Father and of the Son and of the Holy Spirit, and teaching them to obey everything I have commanded you. And surely I am with you always, to the very end of the age."
(Matthew 28:18-20)

Every follower of Jesus is commanded to be baptized. This is not simply a good idea or a great suggestion. It is a command of Jesus. It is a symbolic act of our desire to follow Jesus by identifying with Jesus in His death, burial and resurrection through water baptism. The Apostle Paul wrote concerning baptism…

"Or do you not know that as many of us as were baptized into Christ Jesus were baptized into His death? Therefore we were buried with Him through baptism into death, that just as Christ was raised from the dead by the glory of the Father, even so we also should walk in newness of life."
(Romans 6:3-4 NKJV)

Baptism is our identification with Jesus and the outward symbol of our inward commitment. If you are a follower of Jesus and have asked Jesus to forgive you of our sins, then your responsibility is to obey Jesus by being baptized.

4 – DO I HAVE TO BE BAPTIZED IMMEDIATELY AFTER MY CONVERSION?

There are some groups that teach you must be baptized immediately after praying to receive Jesus or you are not truly a Christian. I do not believe the New Testament supports this view. Certain people in the New Testament were baptized immediately. Those that responded to Peter's message on the Day of Pentecost in Acts 2 were baptized at the moment of their conversion. In other instances, such as in the case of the Apostle Paul, who was converted on the road to Damascus, was not baptized for at least three days when his sight returned to him. The point is that baptism does not have to be immediate, but it should not be left to the backburner either. If you have decided to follow Jesus, then follow His example and be baptized.

5 – DOES IT MATTER WHERE I AM BAPTIZED?

Churches over the ages have used a myriad of venues to conduct baptisms. Formal baptisteries, rivers, oceans, lakes, streams, swimming pools, Jacuzzis, and bathtubs have all been used to baptize those that wish to obey the Lord in this act. I believe all of these venues and many more are valid. The issue is not how "holy" the water is, but how sincere the person entering the water is. If a person gets married on the beach and not in a church, is their marriage still valid? Of course it is! You could get married in a zoo and it would still be valid because we understand that the issue is not the location, it is the condition of the heart and the sincerity of the faith that is being professed.

6 – AM I NOT A CHRISTIAN IF I DON'T GET BAPTIZED?

Baptism is not a prerequisite for heaven, nor are we saved through baptism. The act of going into the water doesn't save us. Jesus saved you through His death on the cross and resurrection from the dead. When we place our faith in His finished work, it is at that moment that we are saved.

"For if you confess with your mouth that Jesus is Lord and believe in your heart that God raised him from the dead, you will be saved. For it is by believing in your heart that you are made right with God, and it is by confessing with your mouth that you are saved."
(Romans 10:9-10 NLT)

We are saved through faith, not any works that we do.

"For by grace you have been saved through faith, and that not of yourselves; it is the gift of God, not of works, lest anyone should boast."
(Ephesians 2:8-9NKJV)

To believe that baptism saves us is to believe in a Gospel that our works make us right with God. That is not the case according to Scripture. Baptism does not save you, but the saved are baptized. A person that has truly decided to follow Jesus will obey Him. If one of His commands is to be baptized, then we should obey Him, not because we believe it will save us, but because we believe that our obedience please God.

7 – WILL I NOT GO TO HEAVEN IF I AM NOT BAPTIZED?

"Then one of the criminals who were hanged blasphemed Him, saying, "If You are the Christ, save Yourself and us." But the other, answering, rebuked him, saying, "Do you not even fear God, seeing you are under the same condemnation? And we indeed justly, for we receive the due reward of our deeds; but this Man has done nothing wrong." Then he said to Jesus, "Lord, remember me when You come into Your kingdom." And Jesus said to him, "Assuredly, I say to you, today you will be with Me in Paradise."
(Luke 23:39-43NKJV)

The thief on the cross was not baptized and yet was given the promise of eternal life by Jesus. So baptism is not required for a person to go to heaven. Yet I do believe that if the thief on the cross was told that there was new evidence and that he could go free, I believe he would have been baptized. The fact that he did not have the opportunity to be baptized does not create an excuse for those of us who have the opportunity to obey God. A person with moments to live who calls out to God can have the assurance of salvation as this thief did, yet that should not inspire laziness or idleness in following the teachings of Jesus. Every person who has the ability to be baptized should be, not because heaven depends on it, but because it is an expression of love for our Savior who died for us. The least we can do is obey Him in this simple, yet powerful act.

8 – CAN I BE RE-BAPTIZED?

On occasion, people who were baptized, but then fell away from the faith afterward have asked me this question. Their desire is not to find out if their baptism still "counts", but if they could be baptized again and demonstrate to God their desire to follow Him. Due to the fact that nothing appears in Scripture that would forbid this act, I encourage them to do what they believe God has put in their heart. Many times, tears flow as the person enters the water and is baptized for a second time. I personally experienced this. I had not fallen away from the faith. Instead, I felt God calling me to begin a new chapter in my life by planting Calvary Fellowship. I was in Israel at the time baptizing people in the Jordan River, when I turned to the Pastors I was baptizing with and asked them to pray for me and baptize me because I wanted to obey God wherever He called me. It was an important moment in my life and one that I believe pleased God.

9 – WHAT IF I WAS BAPTIZED AT ANOTHER CHURCH?
DOES MY BAPTISM STILL COUNT?

Baptism is not about location, but about the presentation of my life to God in obedience to His Word. I recognize that some churches believe you must be baptized in their church for it to truly "count", I believe that the Scriptures teach that baptism is about your relationship with God, not a local church. If you were baptized in one church and then later moved, your baptism has not changed in the eyes of God.

10 – DO I HAVE TO LIVE A PERFECT LIFE ONCE I AM BAPTIZED?

This issue is, can you live a perfect life? I don't think so. Besides Jesus, no person on planet has done it yet. You were not perfect prior to your baptism and you will not be perfect afterwards. Baptism is not where your sins are forgiven. Your sins were forgiven at the cross of Jesus when you placed your faith in His finished work. The Bible says, *"If we say we have no sin, we are only fooling ourselves and refusing to accept the truth. But if we confess our sins to him, he is faithful and just to forgive us and to cleanse us from every wrong."* (1 John 1:8-9 NLT) You are not expected to be perfect after your baptism. I'm sorry to break the news to you, but you will still be the same sinner who entered the water when you exit it. However, you will have taken one huge step: the step of obedience. I have learned that when I can obey God in the small things, following Jesus in the bigger issues of life aren't as difficult. So while you will not be perfect once you are baptized, it will probably mark a time when you got serious about the things of God and your relationship with Him.

11 – WHAT'S THE DIFFERENCE BETWEEN WATER BAPTISM AND THE BAPTISM OF THE HOLY SPIRIT?

"For John baptized with water, but in a few days you will be baptized with the Holy Spirit... But you shall receive power when the Holy Spirit has come upon you; and you shall be witnesses to Me in Jerusalem, and in all Judea and Samaria, and to the end of the earth."
(Acts 1:5,8 NIV)

Water baptism is our identifying with Jesus' death, burial, and resurrection (Romans 6:3-4). The Baptism of the Holy Spirit is a spiritual empowering that is given to each believer in Jesus for works of service. The baptism of the Holy Spirit is when God gives spiritual gifts to His people so they can be His witnesses all over the earth. What type of power is Jesus referring to? The word translated "power" is the Greek word "dunamis", where we get our English words, "Dynamite" and "Dynamic". This power transformed the disciples of Jesus from men who were living in fear of their lives to men who were risking their lives of the sake of Gospel. How does a person receive this power? All that it takes to receive this power is to pray and ask God to empower you. Let Him know that you want to be His witness in this world and that you want to live for Him. There might not be any flashing lights and you may not have any emotional reaction at all, but watch what God does. If you ask to be filled with the Holy Spirit and be empowered by the Holy Spirit, He will do it!

12 – WHAT DOES IT MEAN TO BE BAPTIZED FOR THE DEAD? IS THAT BIBLICAL?

Some cultic groups practice this ritual and use this one verse (out of context) to prove their position on this practice.

"Otherwise, what will they do who are baptized for the dead, if the dead do not rise at all? Why then are they baptized for the dead?"
(1 Corinthians 15:29NKJV)

Mormons call this practice "baptism by proxy" and it is completely unbiblical. They miss the simple meaning of the text and force an interpretation that does not fit the context of what the Apostle Paul is communicating. Paul's point in 1 Corinthians 15 is that if Jesus did not rise, then we are pitiful people at best. So when he gets to verse 29, he says what benefit is there for a person to be baptized if the dead (the person he is referring to here is Jesus) don't rise. If Jesus didn't rise from the dead, then we are being baptized for the sake of the dead and this makes no sense. In fact, to further prove the point, look at Paul's next words:

"And as for us, why do we endanger ourselves every hour? I die every day—I mean that, brothers—just as surely as I glory over you in Christ Jesus our Lord. If I fought wild beasts in Ephesus for merely human reasons, what have I gained? If the dead are not raised, "Let us eat and drink, for tomorrow we die."
(1 Corinthians 15:30-32 NIV)

He says there's no point in living the Christian life if Jesus didn't rise, so there's definitely no reason to be baptized for a person who is dead. But then he makes this triumphant statement:

"The sting of death is sin, and the strength of sin is the law. But thanks be to God, who gives us the victory through our Lord Jesus Christ. Therefore, my beloved brethren, be steadfast, immovable, always abounding in the work of the Lord, knowing that your labor is not in vain in the Lord."
(1 Corinthians 15:56-58NKJV)

What we do is not in vain because Jesus is risen from the dead. That is why our baptism has significance, because we identify with Jesus is His death as we enter the water, then we burst out of the water in newness of life (Romans 6) like Jesus did at His resurrection.

NOTES:

NOTES:

elements

starting a revolution in your world

Available Now

To purchase additional copies or for inquiries:

Phone: 305.822.7000
Web: www.calvarywired.com
Email: info@calvarywired.com

Printed in the United States
102048LV00001B/222/A

9 780977 204724